BONE STRINGS

Also by Anne Coray

Poetry Chapbooks

Undated Passages
Ivory
Soon the Wind

BONE STRINGS

poems by

Anne Coray

Scarlet Tanager
BOOKS

Author and Cover Photos: Steve Kahn
Cover Design: Anne Coray
Graphic Design and Layout Consultant: Solomon Graphics

Published by Scarlet Tanager Books
P.O. Box 20906
Oakland, CA 94620
www.scarlettanager.com

Library of Congress Cataloging-in-Publication Data

Coray, Anne.
 Bone Strings / by Anne Coray.
    p. cm.
 ISBN 0-9670224-9-5
 1. Alaska—Poetry. I. Title
 PS3603.07315B66 2005
 811'.6—dc22
                                    2005004451

For
Claudine Hélène Wiesmann
John Crider Coray

For
Sarah Flowers

For
Steve

ACKNOWLEDGMENTS

Many of these poems, some in slightly different form, appeared in the following publications:

Albatross, The Bitter Oleander, Black Dirt, Bogg, Diner, Dry Creek Review, Fine Madness, Green Mountains Review, G.W. Review, Ice-Floe, International Poetry Review, Kalliope, Kestrel, Nimrod, Northwest Review, Pemmican, Poet Lore, Potomac Review, Rattapallax, Rhino, The Southern Review, Sou'wester, Sulfur, Yefief.

"From What Col" appeared as "New Image" in *Sulfur*.
"Beach Walk: Kenai Bluffs" appeared as "Vigilance" in *Kalliope*.

"Word Problem" first appeared in *North American Review*.

Some of these poems appeared in chapbook form, under the following titles:

Undated Passages (published through a grant from the Alaska State Council on the Arts)
Ivory (Anabiosis Press)

Anthologies:
"Becoming the Moon" and "Directions" in *Hunger Enough: Living Spiritually in a Consumer Society* (Pudding House).
"Beneath Sleeping Lady" in *Poems for the Mountains* (Salt Marsh).
"Etymological Travelogue" in *Hymns to the Outrageous* (Pudding House).

"One March Animal's Desire" was selected for the *Verse Daily* web site.

The author wishes to thank The Rasmuson Foundation for its generous support, as well as The Alaska State Council on the Arts, Lucy Lang Day, and poets Ruth Holzer, Mike Burwell, and Tom Sexton.

CONTENTS

III

I

The sun visits cesspools without being defiled.

—Diogenes

TO A FATHER, LOST

Maybe it wasn't that way, the way I imagined:
the nose of your plane diving clean
as a cormorant into the water.
Maybe it was conspicuous, clumsy, the obscene
floundering of an insect, whose damaged wings
slacken and drag, useless, after its sinking body.

Drowning is not kind to the body.
They never found yours—just as well. The image
I keep is my own, sheltered, much as a bird's wings
shelter a nest. I skipped ahead to your skeleton, clean,
unbroken—almost composed, a mise en scène
suspended indelibly beneath the water.

Animals near death are drawn to water.
I remember my dog, sunken eyes, bloated body,
collapsed and panting near the river. Things we've seen
cancel so thoroughly the imagination.
Or not. Sometimes they open a window: shatterproof, clean,
one that can never trap dust or dash a sparrow's delicate wings.

At thirty-five feet, your plane had a wing-
span five times an eagle's. Did you fear the water?
Perhaps you never saw it, only felt its clean
tongue lick your hair, your neck, your body,
as you hung, inverted, not yet gasping, images
of your life striking the surface of your mind's blank screen.

Some pictures are better left unseen,
or undeveloped. But even the darkrooms of our lives have wings
we can take as exits, where the transposition of images
slowly arrives, not unlike water
that washes so gently the skin of a stiffening body.
There is a holiness to being clean.

We must believe in this, for the pains we take to clean
our dead, our houses, our air...it's how we retouch the scene—
how I sometimes recover you at night, your body
the body of a long-necked crane, winging
its way northward. Below you the water
casts back the photographic glint of your image.

Nothing is cleaner than the extended wings of birds.
I've seen them rise and dip, rhythmic as wind-stirred water,
unclaimed by the weight of the body. You must have known that image.

ONE MARCH ANIMAL'S DESIRE

Warm days, we punch the snow with our footsteps,
leaving the nights' cool mercury to harden a crust.
Better to travel early, before the sun sends down
the weight of its heat. If we were otters—so light and slick—
surface wouldn't matter. We'd slide, equally happy, over
white wallow, ice or berm.

Slung so low, we would not long for a pelvic vault,
conceive ourselves the surrogates of a god.
Heads up, one arm wrapped around heaven,
the other aping the ground, we're tread-fools
of evolution. It's not that great, this awkward posture
that lumbers, drills and pocks. *Texture,*

some claim, but I'd as soon leave a glaze
or gentle indentation. I want to pass through smoothly,
no belt at the hip, no buckle. One tawny hair
in my wake where my belly runnels the snow,
or a slender whisker dropped in woods
as I make my way to the river.

HERACLEUM LANATUM (Cow Parsnip)

The flowers seem whiter this summer,
more delicate than I remember:
drops of ethereal blood,
the umbels an onionskin tracing
set down with a fine-tipped pen.

What else might I miss in this life—
how many days have I not seen the sky,
soft rags of clouds shining up the blue,
their shadows tumbling casually
over the mountains, while disillusion

like a dark flame burned
my mind's petty length.
I'm tired of human clamor,
smudge and clutter of the world.
Who wants to go on
governed by the same rude horns,
the demagogues, the rabble?

Let the culture fall to its own cravings;
I'm taking up with things divine:
leaf-filter, sheath and fiber,
stalks so tall they often lean
but determine to grow taller,
that ask for only the rain's thin coins,
the soil's nutrient and a decent light.

SCRIMSHAW

It's more than patience—
it's the recognition that the ship
doesn't make entirely the scene

it's the *scritch scritch scritch*
the song the artist sang
as he etched the sea, the sails

how he could distinguish the lubber from the mate
and allow the hunt *scritch scritch*
was something greater than the whale

another tool, a different angle
by which he could render
the hull, each plank

seasoned *scritch* then slowly steamed to fit
and held with hand-forged nails
or pegs in place   so he imagined

the rigging, the vast reticulate
of line condensed on the ivory *scritch*
the tooth *scritch scritch*

and in his heart the fibrous hemp
was all the strength that steadied his arm,
his fingers *scritch*

as moments became a mist and smells
a distant breeze that carried wings
and the warmth of moorings *scritch*

designs (were they feathers
or arrows?)—laid down at last
and curving slightly *scritch* like surfaces

of worlds, of signatures: all echoes
for the silent ink

COMMON MEASURES

If you listen long to the waves
you will learn to measure distance,
broad strum of wind from the valley,
short pluck and pick from the lake's edge.

*

Those mornings when a wing of light
glides up above the bay we watch.
We talk: nothing much. Last night was cool.
The lake is calm. We've berries still to harvest.

*

Dinner: potatoes, grouse, and lettuce and dill
from the garden. Preparing it, I ask,
"Is meaning synonymous with worth?" "Some questions,"
says my husband, "sure make a slow salad."

*

September twenty-fourth. The swans and geese are leaving.
Which ones fly first? Are they nervous or wiser?
To the north, a joining of snow
to mountains more luminous than a church.

*

Port Alsworth: one hundred resident Baptists.
We're thirteen miles away, and staying. In summer,
dust from the airstrip toils upward and stalls;
a pterodactylic signature of souls.

*

History's full of false holds, like this lake
dubbed over, named for Clark. He only passed through once,
with a reporter. *Qizhjeh Vena,*
the Dena'ina called it. "Many peoples gather."

*

We live on sacred ground. Brown Carlson, long gone,
buried his first wife on this plot, and up the hill
a circle of stones for my brother Paul.
O curse us spirits, if we so close, not visit.

*

Mountain cloud, solo drummer. We can't beat joy out.
It comes sometimes in the form of color:
rose on scarp and peak just west of Copper,
backdrop rhythm of sky, blue-violet.

*

Soon it will snow, and rosehips outliving the last
glow of summer won't survive the storms. Memory,
dried stem, works hard to remember them, like breath,
urging the late night coals to a color almost translucent.

GROUNDED

Summer's thick graft,
fibrous air.
Tongues sluggish, drunk
with wild rose.

There is no lift
from corporeal musk.
Lamb, baked bread,
perfume of fat and honey.

Sinking muscle,
stuck wing.
Hot fly hum.
The season's canticle,
the heavy soul.

ARS POETICA

Nothing can be said
that is intended.

You cannot grow melons
but you learn that swamp grass
is of equal value.

If you should exact
the sound of a dove
you are perhaps unfortunate.
The coo must become
something slightly
undefined and private.

Deference to the self
is the only way to patience.
Is the slug unhappy
because he has no followers?

If you believed once in water
(whether oceans or tears)
you will someday uncover salt.
You will learn how it is mined,
begin a study of structure.

Curiously, you'll find the tongue
reluctant to accept a formal logic.

What you tend, after all,
is invariably simple:
a leaf, a blade, a stone,
the vowels long and pure,
rich and lovely.

OPEN WATER

Impossible to imagine
the merganser's breast,
settled against a liquid
close to frozen.
November cuffs the mercury
down, down, but there's wind enough
to keep a curve of wave
                —painful undulation—

Maybe the tough get tougher,
I don't—chilblains
around the knuckle, goose bumps
a summons to turn in,
wash dishes, fold towels, take up
a pas-de-deux with the dust
on my kitchen shelves.

The bird's still visible
from my window.
A female, mop-headed,
she swirls, then plunges,
looking for any gullible fish.
I catch my breath.

Inside, and still I shiver,
feeling the water
parting to her beak,
serrated scissor the color of blood
that crushes the fingerling's white flesh.
I prefer not to think of her like this.

I've stopped my cleaning,
moved to the bigger window.
The merganser's gone.
In a month she'll seek

salt water, the surface of this lake
yielding to a quiet clap of ice.

There is no charity,
even in the noon's gloved palm.
I need to go out again,
collect firewood, bank snow
around the cabin.
I'll put on my mittens and down coat,
trap in my little wisdoms, my little heat.

MOCK RIVER

Another morning's landlocked story.
Another morning abiding the hook and the line.
The jays have been up for hours, scouting
the beach for salmon, remnants mostly,
already stripped and scattered by the bears.
Meanwhile, clouds build to a rubber erasure.
The trees slough off their last dead leaves.

Jesus, it's tiring, dog whine and dénouement,
tongue-sweeper, pulling its own weight under.
But you don't give up. You log in: *Waded out.*
Plumbed the shallows for a turned pebble,
one syllable's radiant spawn.

THE ORIGIN OF INSTRUMENTS

I

Voice, some say, was first, and it kindled melody
that licked the mind's dark rock with silver fire.
Bright star, as it evolved, became a hum wet-hot,
ran crooning past her child and on
until her mouth assumed the shapes
of various forest bells. Was that named then singing?
And who came to sit beside her, hand-stick
drumming his thigh—a lover or brother?

II

Frank Livingstone would have it less romantic.
Even before full speech, *Australopithecus africanus*
yodeled across the wide savanna
in pursuit of meat; when his crude pebble tools
crushed the bones of some lumbering beast,
he song-called his fellows to dinner.

III

The loon knows better.
It tells of a reed, slender neck snapped
by the wrist of a furious wind
that departed then swift to a high mountain,
of a silence frail as silk
and the kinsman who rose from a darkening pond
blew his light breath softly over the body—
tones so hollow even the stars began to throb
in the gold and lonely register of grief.

DIVESTED

The mist,
a perfume of absence,
walks through the day's largess.

I have nothing.
No tonic of bright bells,
or resound of iron.

A casket meant for pearls
drifts on the mute wind.

ELEGY FOR FOUR WOLVES
KILLED BY A NEIGHBOR LAST DECEMBER

The north wind strums its bone strings.
Ravens too make their music, plucking
the last fish scraps from the ice.
And I am still worrying transitions,
stuck in a brutal month of blood and skins.
It is April. The snow has scarcely melted.
If language were so easy, it would bear
me a new instrument, one that can't be tuned
to these fibrillary notes of sorrow. Or better,
it would be its own composer, who slips
down thirteen miles of lakeshore to stir
a sleeper's ear with its song. *Pianissimo.*
While at another house, in another season,
dusk returns to untrouble the tracings
of a poor score.

THE SEA COW

Her heavy body heaved away from shore,
a sprout of blood on her back, where the last gash furrowed.
A plague of knives and bayonets, pennons of loosened skin
rippled in clear May air, the fluked anchor
gouged her side. Men on beach and boat held firm.
She weakened. Her mate, clubbed and jabbed, swam in
as far as the shallows. *Food for a fortnight*, wrote the lieutenant.

Seven months the shipwrecked crew had fought:
scurvy, foxes, weather and starvation.
Forty would survive, not Bering. He died December eight,
half-buried already in sand. Discredited, scorned,
he'd given ten years to the Crown, an ever-listing ship
of duties. He was tired. He cared no more for honor.
Briefly, he'd seen his men loosen their insolent
lines of rank, to tend one another as friends.
At the edge of his dreams, the sea cow nibbled the tender kelp,
quietly, as if kindness could be a way of life.

DECEMBER RAIN

In time, friendship will disabuse you.
There will be no one left who has not promised
a stretch of road then bequeathed to you
a winter thicket of wild roses.

You will become accustomed
to December rain that should have been snow,
as you will adjust to the strange warmth
that tenders your fingers when they are strafed with thorns.

Counting on no gunner of a sun to open fire
on cloud and storm, you'll learn to accept
that loyalty is not a character of nature.
The human thumb is less

opposable than you had supposed.
So be it; hold to nothing.
Even your own words may turn against you,
the troubadour's string no longer astounding,

its music undermined by the current drip
that swindles the heart of a former love.
As for epitaphs, let the wind efface them,
blank stone as close to anything that should assume our trust.

II

Lighter than air

                  Than water

Than lips

        Light light

Your body is the footprint of your body

—Octavio Paz, "Transit"

BENEATH SLEEPING LADY (Mount Susitna)

Night rests on this mountain
like a great thigh.
You have said a woman's breast is a moon
and her mouth a sweet river.
I am, as usual, cold.
My hands seek an accustomed warmth
inside your jacket.
Again we've stood our glass up to the stars
and named the constellations.
Sometimes I wonder how we go on
loving the familiar and the magnified.

INTERIORS OF THE IMAGE

I

The mind opens and shuts.
A clearing, a spring robin.
A doe nuzzling her dead fawn.

The desk lamp's perfect angle.
The particular drape of a robe.

We live inside this house.
The image lives inside us.

II

What we take for our own:
Rilke's angels. Jeffers' hawks.

I turn to the curtains.
Their vertical splendor.
The grace of the arch.
The blank finality of sky.

III

Motion must come slowly.
The circling gulls.
Shadows gently sifted
by the sun.

There are things
I just begin to know:
how the stillness of objects
makes more beautiful their bodies.

FOOFARAW

The wind is not rude or indifferent, and even
as I delight in the minor drama of appositives,
I feel unlawful. Why make this April snow
a pockmarked body or the sun a governing eye?
Can we love the hill if it is not anatomical?

Now chickadees are at the feeder, wearing their
black caps and bibs. Ridiculous? Yes. But
how compelling is the jay if it is merely gray?
Or the goshawk simply northern?

Our signatures are written in the tracks of rabbits,
our punctuations in the shapes of rain. The road-
side spruce won't care if we call them honest;
I think there is no guilt or innocence
in the fervency of wanting to belong.

ETYMOLOGICAL TRAVELOGUE

hob
       today that's all
  I like it
  I look it up

  (now that's a funny idiom
why not down,
around, through?)

but here:

   1. a shelf or projection
     at the back or side
     of the inside of a fireplace,
     for keeping things warm

so prepositional and cozy
takes us back (up?)
to this little Irish cottage
made of stone

          been there?
back implies you have
but let's assume we've all
taken the figurative side-trip

it's nice here, mossy and overgrown
and there's some bird—
probably a lark—at the window
it's spring,

you've made a new acquaintance,
a country bumpkin (Dutch? "little tree," squat)
who is anything but—
he's tall, and you can
call him handsome if you want

26

what's relevant
is his friendliness

in fact, everything is friendly: the hearth,
the pot of tea, the hob

and you even allow that little

   2. sprite or elf

to visit
and tell of *his* troubles—

how old Mrs. O'Shaughnessey
has been canceling his magic with her red onions

applied as a poultice for acne,
arthritis and congestion
and how the damn shamrock
is taking over his meadow—

all you can do is smile
because this world
is of unknown origin
but has something to do
with a man you met
(Robert or Robin?)
and anyway,
you're on vacation.

ALASKAN BORN

This foal that is my love
lies in high grass, discovering
heartbeats, wild iris,
tongues, breath, celery, hair,
wetness, spears.

The earth,
warm with our moisture,
is scented with the crush
of violets and skin.
Seeds that have lain long
rush past willows and birches,
to search the alp lily's bed.

This lush growth
is a late telling,
but I will be one day standing
in pastures of deep-rooted promises,
arthritic, delicate at the withers,
with you, nuzzling.

FALL EQUINOX REUNION

All talk
churns softly
in this folded room,
turns golden, thick
as skimmed
and ripened cream.

An evening together,
weaving the family's
homespun threads—
laughter, fingertips,
a twill of amber light.

There is fresh-baked bread
with jelly of the season.
Currants spread
their cloudless luminance;
about the gathering,
the ruby glow.

AN AFTERNOON

The fireweed smile,
pink and eager.
Flies drone.
The Rohn River
twists its gray plait
over boundless stones.

Today your mouth
is filled with vowels.
I want to reach
down your lovely throat
and pull them out.

I make an imaginary lei
with the o's and a's.
My wishes are tropical
and sticky like poi.

Kiss my tangerine-
sweetened lips,
my wild hibiscus thighs.
Our hair will comb
the grasses and the clover.

The sun,
in its highest hour,
will infuse the feltleaf
willow, impart to its skin
a lingering heat.

AND THIS LATE VOW

Love, let me not speak to you of changes.
If a stubborn stoop has unmeasured your height

by a heartless inch, I decline to notice.
July seventeenth, full middle of summer,

the birches hang long with leaves.
Strawberries pledge a fat fruit.

I watch you pause just over midway up the path,
in a backdrop of fireweed and roses.

It is our tenth anniversary. Today
the clouds will not dare to snuff

the light's long candle. We'll paddle
our canoe through a chain of marshes,

watch tall wild cotton on thin stems
maneuvering deft currents of wind.

UNLIT

I wake,
see the blackened chimney
of the lamp, the lung
of weighted dreams.

Outside, bats
slice the night.

I want that handling
of vision,
that swift sense
of blind rule
and cleanliness.

AFTER A FASHION

Finally it will be time to rise
and accomplish one small thing—
a stick of wood for the fire,
a look outside to the leaves
that have turned, since morning,
one shade closer to God or gold.
And that's the crux of it,
whether to embellish or strip;
like the wind, I can never gauge
my strength.

How I'd love to muzzle down,
dog-like, to tradition.
Alaska has one kind of master:
solitary, lean, a hunter fleshing hides,
scraping cold and light, honing
a smooth yet cautious stroke.
The ground, covered with stone or marsh
is still, though from it could push
a thin June flower, or a sprig
of silverweed or sedge.
On a southeast ridge,
rain blends songs of the pine-wife.

Yet there are nights
given to things more fabulous:
a flutter of stars in the sky's palm,
the low *whoo whoo*
of the recluse owl,
bats crossing, recrossing
the dark's wide heart.
When the breeze has dropped
a fresh chill moves in
then silence begins its slow spinning,
a thicket of calm
seizing the land's great lung.

And tomorrow?
A little drama in the trees,
wind shifting into fifth,
turned east, sun
burning fog off the bay.
Cirrus to the south, snow
lowering its dragnet
down the mountains; month
of the ample moon, September,
frost-blessed and shimmery—
every determiner is weather.

ALASKAN

Here, death is common by air.
Flights in fog and overloaded planes
take many, and widows lie
in star-laced beds,
the names of the unburied
soft upon their lips.

Years and years of tender burning,
those bright lights gently fade—
names turn slowly
to dust and carbon,
that drift and settle
with memory's dying wind.

So they are given over:

flying Cook Inlet's coast
or a mountain pass,
there are little puffs
that make the airplane shudder,
breaths of the invisible
reclaiming their position
in the sun-washed sky.

ABSENCE I

I know what your coat
isn't without you in it.
It isn't a corpse
or a full moon. It's the hush
consuming the dried cocoon.

ABSENCE II

Without you in it,
your coat is a hollow cast,
a monk's carapace.
The crevasses of its folds:
deep as five centuries.

EIGHT SONGS

Steam fog on the lake,
a five-knot wind—
the clouds shift,
one haunch to another.

*

All month
the wet breath thickens:
too much blindness,
too many dogs.

*

Obscurity has a certain
sexuality. Reaching for it,
one parts
and both are lost.

*

Ground is figure, figure ground.
We hum, but the melody
makes no contour
of the song.

*

North and west
have gone out walking,
hand in hand,
far from the coast.

*

Ah, you women with your plans!
You forget that dreams
are boredom.

*

Ah, men!
You would blame everything
on weather.

*

White recesses,
white doors.
Come back—go.
Come back—follow.

-40°

Nothing rows
through this thick tongue
of shoreless winter.

The mind
is a lodged
skiff's tiller.

White
as the mute ice,
the heart's
arrested hammer.

MAIL RUN

*My mother tried to support us. To get cash, she hauled mail
by dog team from Iliamna to Nondalton, Port Alsworth, and
other locations on Lake Clark.*
            —Andy Balluta, from *Nuvendaltin
            Quht'ana, The People of Nondalton.*

Sophie—I want to know not
simply what you did, but how
you did it, gripped with intent,
each journey spent reading snow.

Fresh, powdered, granular, packed,
slush stuck like wax to runners—
in low woods, on frozen lakes,
as thick flakes fell like letters,

built into drifts by the wind.
How your mind deciphered page
after page of cursive trail,
sharp as the snowhook's steel edge.

THE PTARMIGAN

*—After the accidental shooting of a well-known Anchorage
doctor, Mari D. Koch, by her long-time friend Gleo Huyck.*

This death on my hands,
strung with the rough craftsmanship
of chance, heavy as fetters
iced with rime,

is still unreal.
It happens.

Again I see that body,
not white yet
but turning, wings
soft and desperate, blurred. Quickening
                              skyward.

I step ahead; she falls behind.
The bird is gone, and I,
unbelieving, watch

the gun fall neatly
to the tundra, as if a single
cloud had drawn a shaft
of darkness through the brilliant light.

Cranberries crack underfoot, their skins
unable, in this late season,
to hold anything still liquid.

My boots are stained with blood.

My bullet—my body
                    ricochets
        —forward, back.

Nothing in her face suggests a human face.
Only her mouth, hung
with the inarticulate wisdom
of the dying,
          explains.

How suddenly
everything to me she never was
—wife, mother, sister, child—
she has become.

And I the failed, the hunted.

WAITING

—for my mother

Autumn: drafts already in the cabin.
She played with her baby, swung her up
and down, keeping them both warm.
Then her arms went suddenly limp,
as the strings of an abandoned puppet.
The radio voice cut out, cut in.

"...Coray, pilot...left Friday...passengers...
his son...whereabouts still unknown..."
She stared at the rain, the fog, the rain,
at the net, unmended, hanging in the corner.
She felt the news unraveling the days
like strands of broken filament.
Every hole that gaped at her
was her dying hope
that she could not repair or throw away.

DIRGE

I carried the moose calf back
along our beach, where the rocks
are large enough to make me stumble.

I carried her back—
I judged her the weight
of a small dark cloud—
she was one week old, at most.

I tried at first
to purge the water
from her lungs, her nose.

The calf dashed into our yard
separated from her mother
—a bear between them, we figured—

then swam too far
in the frigid lake
chased by my border collie pup,
who only wanted to play.

When she finally turned,
we heard her whimpers.
Her ears were down,
her swimming slower.

I carried her back from where
she'd almost managed the shore.
I was not even sure if she drowned
or died from shock.

I should have run when I first saw her
toppling like a body gone with drink,

should have pulled her from the water
toweled her coat, offered
a bottle of warm sweet milk.

We thought the mother dead,
the calf just resting
in the shallows.

And what would we have done
with the mother gone
and the tiny thing in a pen—
our own exotic zoo?

I carried the moose calf back
while another question
shaded the foundering, midday sun—
should we eat her?

We laid her down
on our boat's red carpet.
She was such a beautiful, simple brown
her eyes a little milky,
oval as a murre's.

On the smallest island we left her
in alder on the dusty ground.
There was never a fleck of blood.

The mother was standing
when we returned
in water up to her knees.

She did not run
or make a sound,
her head was up

while mine, for days, it hung, it hung
and my tears were loud
but they were not good.

LANDSCAPE IN NOVEMBER

Contradiction is a lever of transcendence.
—Simone Weil

In a meadow of crystal-feathered snow,
in the bright silence of the moon,
I imagine I will go to gather roses,
ice-white blooms that build
on the tips of frozen willows.

And they will burn cold and beautiful
in my hands, my touch renewed,
a numbed awakening
to this great thin space that consumes
all grief and joy.

Immobile soul of the night,
clear and impartial air, proclaiming
nothing but its own sheer echo.
Flowers spread for miles,
invisible and scentless;
already my heart lies empty.

RHYTHMICS

The year I spent alone, I learned some things
Of wind and the undulation of shadows,

Of snowdrifts and the moon's beginnings.
I learned where the creeping jenny grows,

How marten follow thickets of spruce.
I learned to tell time by the lake's level,

Words as they lifted and thinned from disuse.
When I felt the low, periodic pull

For human company, I would go
Visit Charlie, my only neighbor.

His voice, like the river, would shift and flow;
His gestures were the whole notes of the score.

I'd come to read a system of notation,
A music, a subtlety of motion.

JOE

Thirty years single
in a gas can
shingle shack,

coffee
your best
company;

how many
hand-rolled cigarettes
and *Time* magazines
did you stutter to,

how many mornings
smooth a stubbled
trembling chin,
suds over your loneliness
in a tin pan

before winter piled on winter

and your dreams
were gold nuggets,
your spade deep
in the same dark hole?

IN THE MARGIN

Lake Clark: Named in 1891 by reporter A.B. Schanz of the Frank Leslie Illustrated Newspaper expedition for John W. Clark, chief of the Nushagak Trading Post, who "discovered" the lake.

Qizhjeh Vena
"many peoples gather"
long before ink, the lake's
Dena'ina name.

This image, sketched
from the mound
and gorge of tongue:
campfires reflected
in glacial water.

Around them, bodies rise—
aged and unfledged bones,
thick forests, rock-
topped mountains.

Something remains—
a flicker: long undated
passages, the press
of hand-sewn boots

made from skins
of vejex, caribou
k'uhda'i, moose.

IVORY

His grandfather carved from it
sleds and sea mammals,
blessed the animal, the spirit,
that gave the people meat,
bone for harpoon,
blubber for fuel.

The grandson shipped it
wrapped in worn tarpaulin,
netted ten dollars,
two cases and a handshake
per bundle.

What was left of his mother
often ruptured his sleep;
in the spoiled night
he would watch her lie
like a walrus heap

heaving herself on the floor,
as she retched Jim Beam
and lifted her fist,
as if to plunge it, brutally,
into that deep and tuskless void.

KINSHIPS

It is my design, now to wander among the oldest layers
of speech, among the farthest phonetic strata.
                                        —St. John Perse

How easily here
we could begin,
white shale moon
uncloaking the night's great hall.
Pictures of things—
claws of animals, limbs
of trees, reaching
for the wisped breath.
Then the wind-born labials:
mountain, willow, vole.
Bold light, rising, past
fireweed, beach pea and rock
to lake: landscape of tongue,
aspirate and carved vowel.
Behind it all, a gurgling,
the river's throat learning
its earliest course—
          Liq'a Qilanhtnu;
from what spring,
what shower—
the world awash with voice.

III

But when I practiced eyeing
The goal of men,
It iced me, and I perished
A little then.

—Thomas Hardy,
"The Dead Man Walking"

FROM WHAT COL

When January in its thin blanket
filtered blue the coastline
of Tanalian

all that was lost
fluttered in an echo, pale yellow
over the snow's hard crust.

Knee-deep, on an ancient trail
I foundered and fell, face-first.
Tooth cut lip; it bled,

pooled onto the glaze of ice.
The moon was up.
I saw the wings of a red raven,

something flapped and cawed—
purple, and strong,
a mix of night and bird.

GRAIN

grain   grain of memory   is it striated or squiggled
is it rough to the stenciled eye?   *I don't know*   what
lightness in this phrase   what joy of un-being
to gaze at a rope   to hold *curvilinear* and *fiber*
to have that braid woven into your soul   to un-name
everything you ever thought you owned   not skin not hand
not desk not pen   a resurrection of poise and smooth
energy   an un-fracturing an understanding derived
from the source of the well   nothing real is visible

I remember the blind man who touched the sculpture
and said it was warmer on one side than the other
and all we saw was form   division subtraction equations
split like atoms   did we anticipate what would happen?
we have gone too far   I want no particles   no tools
to measure the radius of a star   when all the mystery is gone
we will hang by the thumbs of our dissections   the surgical night
will remove our bones

ELECTION DAY: READING CHEVIGNY
AND THINKING ABOUT REFERENDUM SIX

*A yes vote overturns the state legislature's recent reauthorization
of same-day airborne land-and-shoot wolf hunting that an
overwhelming majority of Alaskans voted to ban in 1996.*
—State of Alaska Election Pamphlet

Someday I will write a poem wholly praise
when light perfects a quiet temple
over the wide, insistent village
and a glad sea wells in the trough of these bones.
Not today. I've finished another history
and know the promyshlennik soul that breeds
in the black thick-blooded bowel.
We vote again on another measure of slaughter,
an old shitik put to sail.
It's not just outcome, but the iron bell
with its iron tongue: *and we shall have dominion...*

Outside, clouds are gathering. Soon it will snow.
There are moments I'd like to walk out,
find a little hill and lie down, and let the sky ferry
me into a land so clean it exacts no witness.

DOLLY

Born July 5, 1996, Dolly resulted from the fusion of a nuclear-free unfertilized egg with a donor cell obtained from the mammary gland of a six-year-old ewe.
—*Remaking Eden,* by Lee M. Silver

Oddly, I never thought of you
as animal, or lamb
(were you ever?),
though you must bleed and bleat:
unsimulated purges
of the flesh and soul.
So the heat from your body
is surely your own,
waxing with the heart's full pump
when you run, then
slackening, as you slow
your pace and stand or graze,
oblivious to the grand dissension
that surrounds you.
And the sun, nesting its
blind rays in your wool,
absolves you: small creature
whose creation
was our first chaste sin.

DIRECTIONS

something
is humping
its mother
in the woods

her only seeds
are stones
released
in a black lava

listen

to where
we are going:

a geology
of dark birth

JUST WEST OF HOME

Cold waves
abrade this granite
to a husk,
an island cave.

Deep inside,
my oar strikes once
the skiff's rib,
the sound walled
in a gutted silence.

To enter
is to know, suddenly,
the stomach of death:

      ghost of a sterile scent,
      drift of a weightless vessel.

INTERIM

—for Mike Burwell

The place from which you used to write is here.
In this leaf, furling and furling its dry palm
until it is lifted with the wind.
There is nothing we can do.
The old metaphors strike three times
and we are left with some vague aroma
of autumn. I read Mandelstam and am thankful
I'm able to sleep—unlike his wife, awake five nights
keeping her eye on the guards.
But something about this life is too easy.
We can't make out the warships.
No human heads wander into distance.
Every day birds match their wings
against our breath. Bleeding,
we wait, aware that waiting is not what we came for.

JANUARY THAW

The world emerges in three shades:
gray, gray-black and a color
that had been white.
But even this is a lie;
the yellows of the sick
tinge the aspen trees, and the birches
are reminiscent of flesh.

It is the wrong time of year for grieving.
We wanted no birthing room for spring,
first steppingstone to death.
Frozen, the land postponed
our betrothal to agony and joy.

TAXIDERMY

I think of snow
light sometimes
as feathers or hair—

one brush down
to ice, glazed eye
pure and dead
as a diamond.

Then the depth, immeasurable,
the kind that is its own auger.

Perhaps it is this casting we desire:
an art so quiet not even the lice
come near it.

One can hardly speak of animals.

Indeed, it has more to do with faith:
the perennial skin, lips, antlers, talons.

TANKA CONTRA NATURA

The moon was never
so foreign, pressed in the car's
cocked side view mirror:
a goitrous egg, a buxom
young woman's nippleless breast.

WORD PROBLEM

With the multiplication of angels came the orders—
nine, according to Dionysius the Areopagite—
seraphim, cherubim, and thrones in the first circle;
dominions, virtues, and powers in the second;
principalities, archangels, and angels in the third.

If the dominions combined with the powers
to form an archangelic throne
that was divided in turn by the virtues,
how many seraphim would be left
to split the principalities
among the cherubim and angels?

(Hint: If that seems a little complicated,
just subtract the remainder
of frogs or birds.)

CLEARING

Leaf-choked, swollen
piles of brush.
The stagnant hour.
A gull
settles its gray wings.

A month of mist
and low ceilings;
what we have cut
has not improved
the view.

We huddle, filled
with a cold ambition,
wanting dust
and freedom from the anchor
of our small revisions.

OCTOBER SNOW

Snow claims the roads and trees;
the quick fever of autumn is over.
The red belt of willows that grows
on the lot next door has brightened
against the white cover.
Today, this is all I need to know,
and I bury our destiny's cold questions.
I am thirty-seven. If I live another
forty years, or fifty, I will look back
to this time when weather was still
no hireling of man, when snow formed
only from the atmosphere's cooled vapor.
For this snow that descends
not to extinguish fires or to insure
a better season for skiers,
I am thankful.

BECOMING THE MOON

Dream of things old and foreign. A medieval
castle. An Eskimo drum. Clasp the trees.
Dance circles. Read a poem.

The moon knows a thousand poems. She reads
them sleeping. Every one is quiet yet equally wild.

Say nothing to the factories, the rivers,
the sick swan. Cast your light, indiscriminate
and cool, on the great machines that sit, so very still,
so innocent, so mortal, in the night.

There is nothing for you but to shine.

WHAT WOULD YOU LIKE TO DO BEFORE YOU DIE?

Well—I'd like to leave
a legacy for the trees,
how they accept what sun they're given,
how they bow to the wind—no matter its direction—
then spring up again, uncomplaining.

I'd like my voice to take on the tone
of the leaves—gold green—I'd like
to recover a silence, patterned after
rings of inner growth.

Although in Barrow now
men are slaughtering walrus,
leaving the meat to a careless rot.
There's money only in the tusks.

I'd like not to have to wonder
if this is even my business.
Or if my language and my life instead of grief
should spend themselves on leavening—

creating a leafy hollow at the base
of my own trunk, where the Swainson's thrush
that hit my window can revive
and build its nest.

Words form, and I'd like to reform them.
I'd like to say:

> Our skeletons are only the half of us.
> There are always the leaves to relieve.

I'd like not to argue
when autumn once again proves me wrong.

RECOVERY

Sometimes it all seems easy:
the old dog lolling in the driveway,
the neighborhood growing quiet,
the April light just fading at 10 p.m.,
the sheets of would-be poems
folded and ready to burn.

You *must* fold them first
because then you may imagine
they are wings
and when the fire takes them
they will lift off
all the way back to that mountain
you tried to climb
far above tree line,
where you wrote that
"nothing here can stand for sorrow—
not the great sky or the hawk,
not lichen, boulders, or moss."

But you didn't believe it then.
Your hopes were for something
still more grand.

Tonight, your greatest deed is done.
Tonight, you give up sorrow.

BEACH WALK: KENAI BLUFFS

Valance of rock,
fine slipper of sand...
the ocean has retreated.
Long strophes of silence
sheen the moist air;

here, the small fingers
of failings and reprisals
loosen,

and one can go on into evening
touching the rough bodies of salt
and watching the light
redefine the shore.

How often does it come to this:
living to wait

until pain climbs out
like a heavenly body
then dissolves...

and it is again possible
to return to the shells and the stones,
to lean outward in the wake
of the storm, to discover
what the tide has salvaged.

THE UNEXALTED

Maria Ivanova, a name almost anonymous
as the star glimpsed, night after night, from the depths
of that black hole she dug for the Motherland,
for Stalin. But she had hope, though the cold
cracked and bit her fingers, and the unseeming end
of twelve hours would earn her only

a kilo of bread—or half—she can't remember. Only
the star kept her going. And work, the anonymous
pick chipping the permafrost, iron to ice, the strokes' unending
rhythm easing a little the shiver of her bones. Depth:
not of heart or despair, but of forty feet. Cold:
not turkey or fish, but a literal stasis of land,

ten inches of frozen soil, no sun for a month. A land
whose copper, platinum and nickel were Russia's only
hope. To build, to prepare for war: infinitives cold
as the soldiers who invented anonymous
crimes, then sentenced the prisoners to forced labor. The depth
of duty measured in years. Ten, for Maria—their end

would leave her not quite thirty. So far off, that end
must have seemed an ephemeral flower, crushed by the land-
scape's flesh-heavy snow. But what choice? Siberia's depths
mocked any notion of flight; from Norilsk, "if onlys"
were snatched from the speaker's lips by a bald, anonymous
wind, or pressed to death by the steel pistons of the cold.

Even summer, with its brief pardon from the cold,
checked one's footsteps. To the west, the Yenesei, at its end
the Kara Sea, and a village all but anonymous.
To the southeast, mountains, but first the impassable marshland.
Yet a city rose from that harsh geography, an only
child, an orphan, and bursting from the depths

of that young heart was music. Music, whose depths
kindled the souls of the guards, as they ate cold
caviar, crab and butter. And drank—not only
vodka, but champagne. Outside, stars spilled like glitter in an endless
sky. Even a prisoner could lift her eyes from the land
and keep her faith in something distant, flawless and anonymous.

It is those depths beyond that make bearable these endless days;
on the coldest nights the stars shine brightest. The land
only collects our grief; the stars release it, untraceable, anonymous.

NIGHT PETALS

I am not sure if they are falling
or burgeoning, because night
is of two persuasions. Call it arrival,
when dusk extinguishes the sun's red flower
and we turn to golden interiors. In this room
the slatted chairs my husband built
recline to a perfect angle. He felled
the birch, milled and planed each board,
sanded and varnished the surfaces.

He sits beneath our propane light
(a quiet light, and cheery)
with his beer and book;
at his feet a tapestry,
its leaves and vines
unchecked by shadows.
Memory, or the mind's own flight
lines this winter womb
with a scene from summer.

He stood with a spade at the edge
of a field—we had come to gather iris—
he knelt; he dug three shoots.
I knew then death as a seed in wind
that would find those holes and flourish.
Those still living would be carried back
to begin again in a new bed.
Let this be our envisioning: the space,
the transfer: green torches ever greening.

NOTES

"The Sea Cow."
Corey Ford, *Where the Sea Breaks its Back* (Seattle: Alaska Northwest Books, 1995).

"Kinships."
Liq'a Qilanhtnu is the Dena'ina Indian name for the Tlikakila River, flowing into Qizhjeh Vena (Lake Clark) in southwestern Alaska.
Linda Ellanna and Andrew Balluta, *Nuvendaltin Quht'ana, The People of Nondalton* (Washington D.C.: Smithsonian Institution Press, 1992).

"From What Col."
Tanalian is the Anglicized version of Tanilen, known today as Port Alsworth.
Ibid.

"Election Day."
promyshlenniki: Free-lance exploiters of natural resources, notably fur.
shitik: The first vessel used in the Russian quest for fur.
Hector Chevigny, *Russian America* (Portland: Binford & Mort, 1985).

"October Snow."
Cloud seeding (also known as weather modification) is the deliberate treatment of certain clouds or cloud systems with the intent of affecting the precipitation process(es)…
—North American Weather Consultants, Inc.

ABOUT THE AUTHOR

Anne Coray lives at her birthplace on remote Qizhjeh Vena (Lake Clark) in southwest Alaska. Her poems have appeared in *The Southern Review, Poetry, Seneca Review, Alaska Quarterly Review* and *Rattapallax,* among others. She has been a finalist with Carnegie-Mellon, Water Press & Media and Bright Hill Press, as well as for the Frances Locke Memorial Award and the Rita Dove Poetry Award. For several years she worked for the Bilingual Program in the Matanuska-Susitna Valley north of Anchorage. She lives with her husband, Steve, and her dog, Zipper.

Also from Scarlet Tanager Books:

Wild One, by Lucille Lang Day
poetry, 100 pages, $12.95

The "Fallen Western Star" Wars: A Debate About Literary California,
edited by Jack Foley
essays, 85 pages, $14.00

Catching the Bullet & Other Stories, by Daniel Hawkes
fiction, 64 pages, $12.95

Visions: Paintings Seen Through the Optic of Poetry,
by Marc Elihu Hofstadter
poetry, 72 pages, $14.00

Embrace, by Risa Kaparo
poetry, 70 pages, $14.00

crimes of the dreamer, by Naomi Ruth Lowinsky
poetry, 96 pages, $16.00

red clay is talking, by Naomi Ruth Lowinsky
poetry, 142 pages, $14.95

Call Home, by Judy Wells
poetry, 104 pages, $15.00

Everything Irish, by Judy Wells
poetry, 112 pages, $12.95